SHANG AND ZHOU DYNASTIES

THE BRONZE AGE OF CHINA
EARLY CIVILIZATION

ANCIENT HISTORY FOR KIDS
5TH GRADE SOCIAL STUDIES

In this book, we're going to talk about the Shang and Zhou Dynasties. So, let's get right to it!

Civilization in the country of China began thousands of years ago. When the rulers passed away their sons or another one of their relatives took power so this is how the dynasties of China began. Prior to the Shang Dynasty, there was the Xia Dynasty, which took place from 2070 BC through 1600 BC.

SCULPTURE OF BUDDHA HEAD, XIA DYNASTY

TOMB, XIA DYNASTY

A lthough, the history of the Xia Dynasty was recorded many centuries after the fact, there have been no archaeological findings to verify that it actually took place. That is why historians sometimes consider the Shang Dynasty the first, since it has both written records and artifact evidence.

THE SHANG DYNASTY
(1600 BC TO 1046 BC)

Around 1600 BC, the Shang people became powerful. They had a leader who was called Cheng Tang. He inspired the people to unite and rise up against the wicked leader of the Xia Dynasty whose name was Jie. Cheng Tang and his people fought against King Jie and won. Then, they established the Shang Dynasty, sometimes called the Yin Dynasty.

CHENG TANG

Their kingdom thrived in the lands of the Yellow River Valley in China for about five hundred years. The rule of the kingdom was passed from father to son and the capital city wasn't always the same. Unfortunately, the government of the Shang Dynasty eventually became dishonest under the leadership of King Di Xin. When governments become corrupt, sometimes the people revolt. The wicked Di Xin was overthrown by Wu from Zhou and the Zhou Dynasty was established.

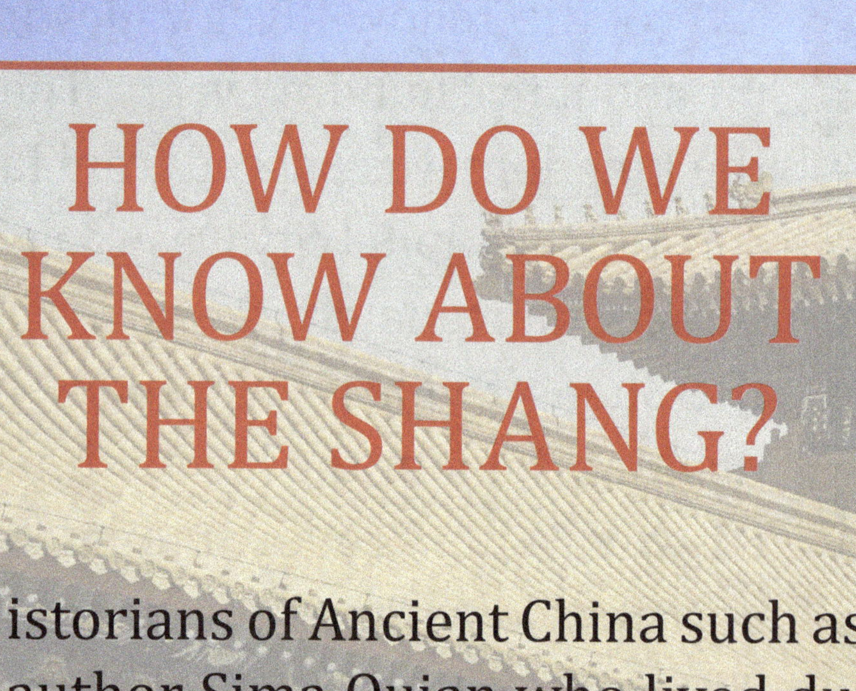

HOW DO WE KNOW ABOUT THE SHANG?

Historians of Ancient China such as the author Sima Quian who lived during the Han Dynasty have written about the Shang Dynasty. Archaeologists have also found short passages that were inscribed on religious artifacts made of bronze.

ORACLE BONE SCRIPTURE

However, most of the information about this dynasty comes from an unusual source. The Chinese spiritual masters used bones to make predictions about the future. These religious men would inscribe a question on one side of the bone, such as "Will we be victorious in battle?" or "Will the king's child be a son?" in order to receive an answer. Then, they would burn the oracle bone until it became cracked.

They would study the cracks to get the answer to their question or the solution to their problem. Then, they would inscribe their interpretation of the answer on the other side of the bone. Archaeologists have found thousands of these special bones, mostly the shoulder bones of oxen or tortoise shells.

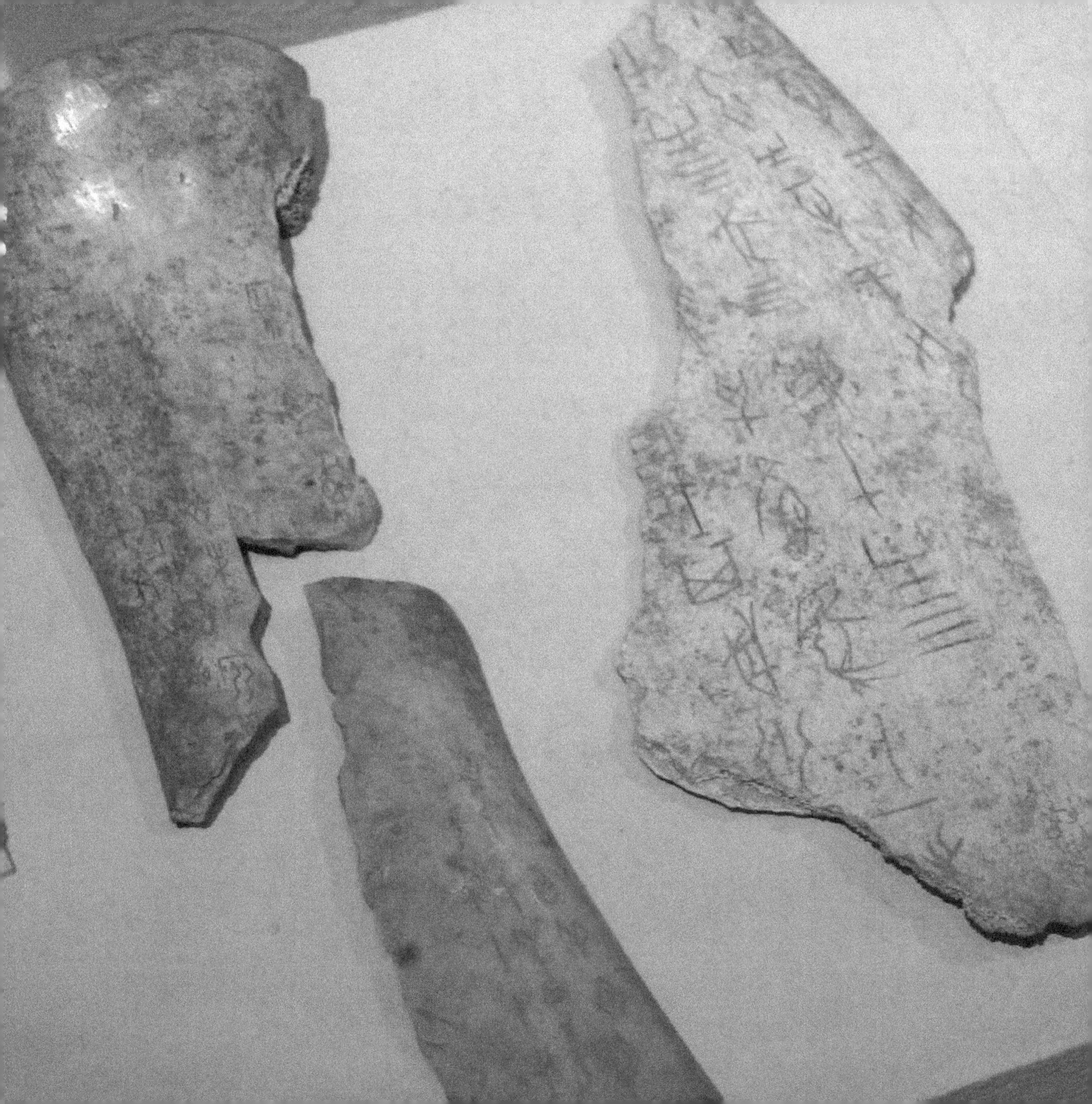

YIN XU

Historians have studied them to piece together the history of the dynasty. Many such bones have been found at the site of Yin Xu, which was the dynasty's last capital city.

SHANGDI TEMPLE

In addition to using the oracle bones to make future predictions, the people of the Shang Dynasty also revered their dead ancestors and paid homage to a divine being who was known as Shangdi.

WRITING DURING THE SHANG DYNASTY

The Shang people were the first Chinese people to create a system of writing. Their ancient script closely resembled modern Chinese characters. Writing was an aid in organizing their government as well as their society.

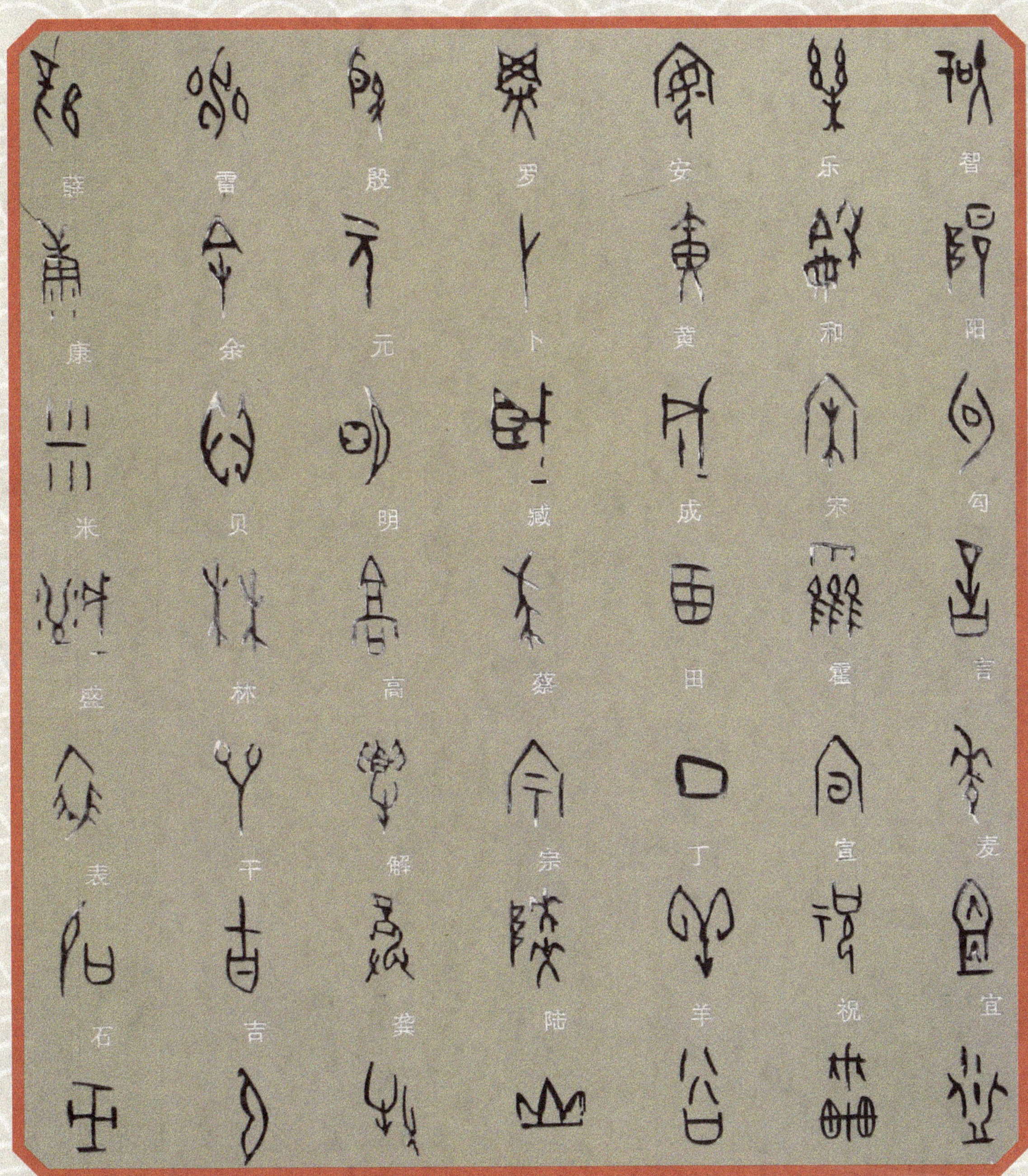

TRADITIONAL CHINESE CALLIGRAPHY

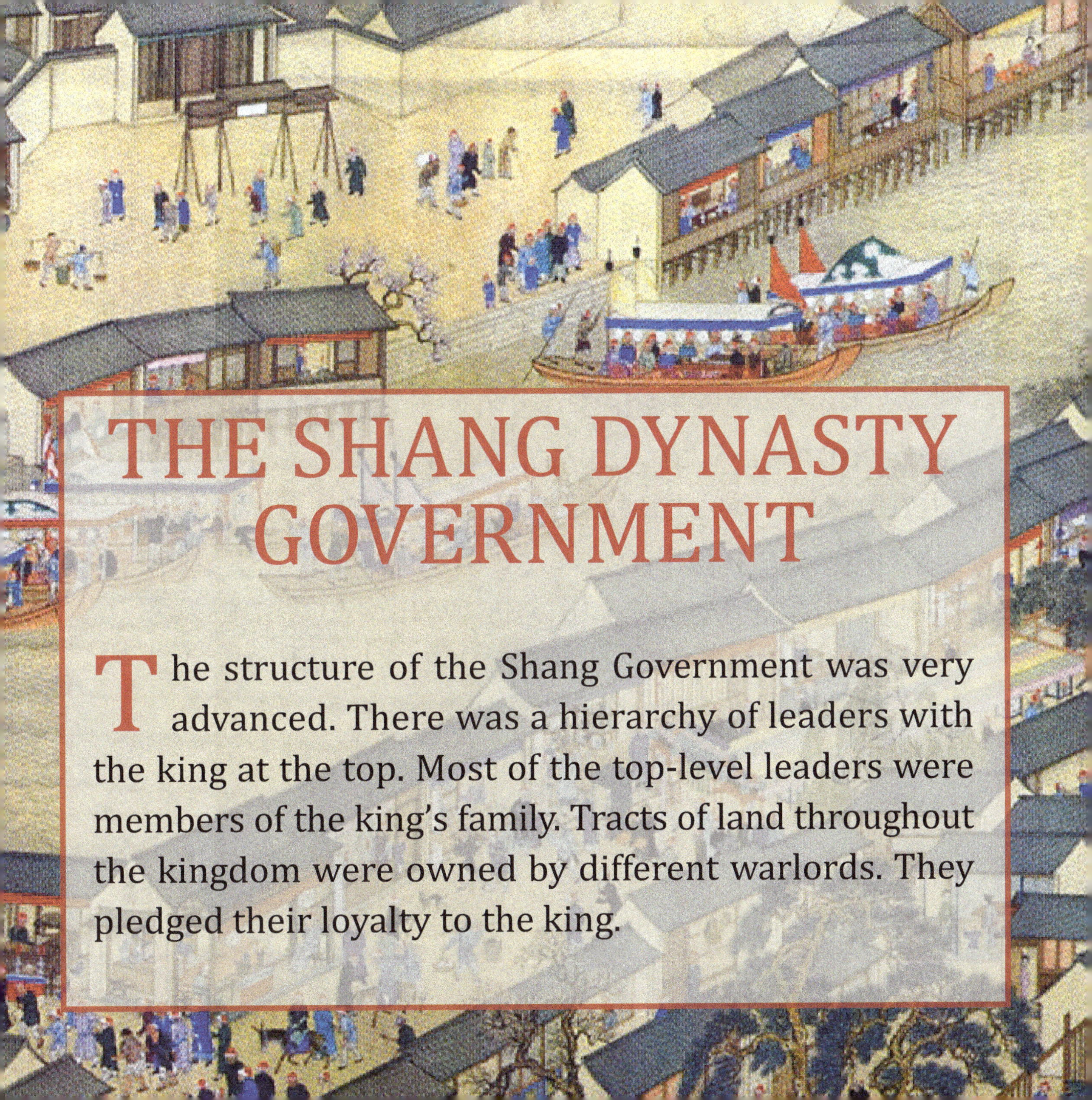

THE SHANG DYNASTY GOVERNMENT

The structure of the Shang Government was very advanced. There was a hierarchy of leaders with the king at the top. Most of the top-level leaders were members of the king's family. Tracts of land throughout the kingdom were owned by different warlords. They pledged their loyalty to the king.

T hey were called upon to supply soldiers during war time. Taxes were collected from the population to run governmental services and surrounding allies were asked to pay tribute to the king as well. Wu Ding was one of the famous kings during the Shang era. He ruled for a span of 58 years.

WU DING

BRONZE TECHNOLOGY DURING THE SHANG DYNASTY

During the Shang Dynasty, craftsmen learned how to create using bronze. They made weapons for war as well as religious items from bronze. The bronze spears they created were very strong and provided

them with an advantage in battle. They also learned to use chariots that were pulled by horses, which provided another advantageous strategy they could use against their enemies in battle.

ZHOU
Qin
Jin
Song
Qi
Chu
Wu
Yue
Shu
Ba
Lu
Wey
Cao
Zheng
Chen
Cai
Dao
Shen
Deng
Tang
Sui
Kui
Yong
Yun
Yiqu
Guifang
Loufan
Di
Dai
Yan
Wuzhong
Guzhu
Zhongshan
Nie
Lai
Xu
Huaiyi
Zhongwu
Zhoulai
Zhongli
Chao
Pu
Luo
E
Viet (Baiyue)
Tan
Gu
Fei
Xing
Li
Huo
Yang
Zhai
Liang
Yi
Huan
Wei
Xi
Ge
Fan
Wang
Wen
Gong
Liu
Hua
Yu
Guo
Mao
Jiao
Jiao
Ruo
Gou
Gu
Mi
Yú
Bao
Jŭ
Cheng
Ying
Xŭ
Hu
Dun
Dài
Xiang
Fan
Xi
Jiang
Lài
Liao
Jiang
Huang
Xian
Zhen
Zeng
Lù
Ying
Shŭ
Tong
L'u
Han
Guo
Suo
Sui
Feng
Zou
Xue
Xiao
Peng
Lú
Tán
Chéng
Mou
Zhōu
Ji
Chunyu
Yí
Zhū
Yang
Ju
Xiang
Bei
Dong

THE ZHOU DYNASTY (1046 BC TO 221 BC)

Of all the dynasties in China's history, the Zhou was the longest time period and lasted 825 years. Zhou was one of the states of the Shang Dynasty. Wen Wang was a powerful commander of this vassal state. He came up with a strategy to overthrow the Shang.

Battles took place over many years and it was finally Wen's son Wu Wang who led the Zhou armies across the width of the Yellow River to overthrow the Shang. They were victorious and began their new dynasty.

WEN WANG

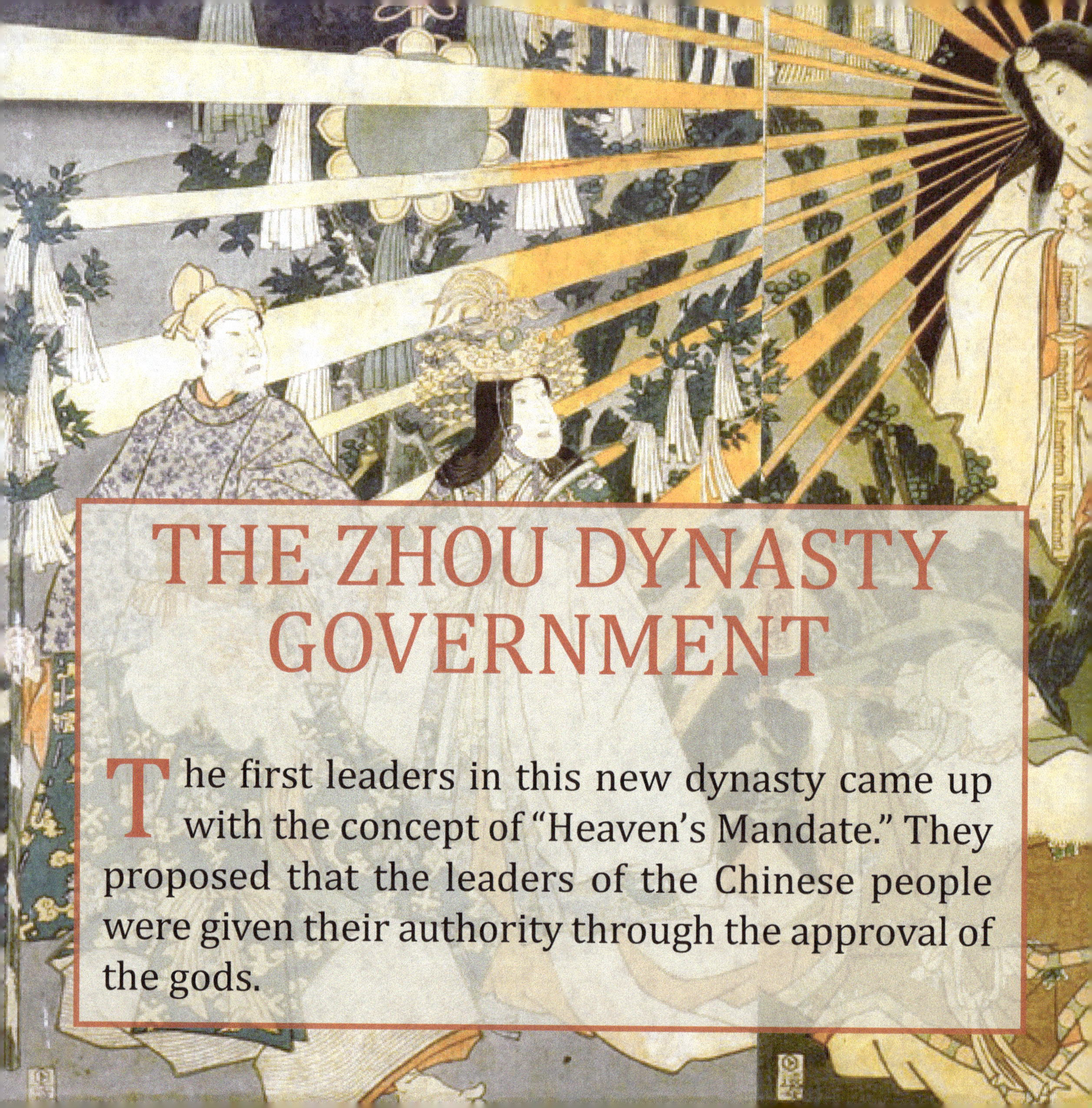

THE ZHOU DYNASTY GOVERNMENT

The first leaders in this new dynasty came up with the concept of "Heaven's Mandate." They proposed that the leaders of the Chinese people were given their authority through the approval of the gods.

HEAVEN'S MANDATE

They firmly believed that the Shang Dynasty had become corrupt and this was why the gods had allowed them to be victorious. Because the Shang leaders had become tyrannical, the gods wished for them to be overthrown.

T he Zhou Government was based on fiefdoms. The king or emperor was at the top of the hierarchy. He separated the land into fiefdoms that were managed and led by his close relatives. They owned the lands so

the lands would stay in the same family. The farmers toiled on the lands to produce the crops, but they didn't own any pieces of it.

孔 子

TWO NEW RELIGIONS

Both the religion of Confucianism and the religion of Taoism developed during this time period. Confucius, the famous philosopher, was born in 551 BC and died in 479 BC. His wise teachings had a huge influence throughout China's history.

A nother philosopher by the name of Lao Tzu introduced Taoism and the concepts of yin, the passive or negative force, and yang, the active or positive force. There are over 6 million people who practice Confucianism today and about 12 million people in the world are Taoists.

CAST IRON GARMENT HOOK WITH GOLD AND SILVER FOIL

TECHNOLOGY ADVANCES DURING THE ZHOU DYNASTY

During the Zhou Dynasty the people figured out how to create cast iron. This made it possible to create very strong tools as well as weapons. Even though iron was important, the Zhou were known for their beautiful work with bronze, which had been introduced during the Shang Dynasty.

Many of the bronze items created during this dynasty had inscriptions on their surfaces. Archaeologists have worked with historians to piece together much of the dynasty's history from these inscriptions. In farming, crop rotation was used to keep the land fertile. Soybeans were introduced as a new crop.

WESTERN ZHOU DYNASTY CARRIAGES

WESTERN ZHOU PERIOD AND EASTERN ZHOU PERIOD

Historians divide the Zhou Dynasty into Western and Eastern periods. The first time period was the Western and was a time of peace and prosperity. Circa 770 BC, some of the Zhou territories rebelled against the king. Lords joined together to fight and they took control of the capital. The Zhou king's son escaped east and once there he established a new capital, which became the Eastern Zhou.

THE SPRING AND AUTUMN PERIOD

Historians call the first years of the Eastern Zhou the Spring and Autumn period. During this time, the feudal lords started to become independent and refused to be controlled by the king. Without the unity of one king, the lords weren't aligned with each other for the greater good and they began to fight amongst themselves. By the end of the dynasty, only seven states remained due to all the fighting.

BRONZE, EASTERN ZHOU DYNASTY

THE PERIOD OF THE WARRING STATES

From 475 BC to the end of the dynasty in 221 BC, there were endless battles among the seven remaining states. The battles were fought under strict, formal rules and the soldiers fought with chivalry and honor. However, it was clear that they would battle it out until one of the states was victorious over all the others. Qin Shi Huaung, who was the Qin state's leader was ultimately the winner.

He conquered all the others and became emperor of the new united China. It's not surprising that the book The Art of War by the author Sun Tzu was written during this dynasty. It is still used today as a metaphor for business strategy.

SUN TZU

ห้ามโยนเหรียญลงบ่อมังกร
...าพสตรีใส่เสื้อ...เดียว
ชุดนุ่งสั้นเหนือ...
...ผ้าคลุมก่อนขึ้น...

SUMMARY

The Chinese mythology stories were supposedly followed by the Xia Dynasty, however no artifacts from this dynasty have been found. The Shang Dynasty came next and there are written records and artifacts from this dynasty, which lasted from 1600 BC to 1046 BC. The Zhou Dynasty began in 1046 BC and lasted until 221 BC.

It was the longest dynasty in Chinese history. Both dynasties were known for their bronze work. Inscriptions on oracle bones and items made in bronze that were inscribed have offered clues about the people who lived during these dynasties.

A wesome! Now that you've read about the Shang and Zhou Dynasties, you may want to read more about ancient Chinese mythology of the rulers before the Xia Dynasty in the Baby Professor book The Three Demigods, The Five Emperors and the Chinese Dragon.

Visit
BABY PROFESSOR
EDUCATION KIDS
www.BabyProfessorBooks.com
to download Free Baby Professor eBooks
and view our catalog of new and exciting
Children's Books